MW00760708

BLACKSNAKE
AT THE
FAMILY
REUNION

Southern Messenger Poets

Dave Smith, Series Editor

BOOKS BY DAVID HUDDLE

POETRY

Glory River
Grayscale
Summer Lake: New and Selected Poems
The Nature of Yearning
Stopping by Home
Paper Boy

FICTION

Nothing Can Make Me Do This
La Tour Dreams of the Wolf Girl
Not: A Trio—A Novella and Two Stories
The Story of a Million Years
Tenorman
Intimates
The High Spirits: Stories of Men and Women
Only the Little Bone
A Dream with No Stump Roots in It

ESSAYS

The Writing Habit
Poetry, Fiction, and Essays
A David Huddle Reader

BLACKSNAKE AT THE FAMILY REUNION

POEMS

DAVID HUDDLE

LOUISIANA STATE UNIVERSITY PRESS

BATON ROUGE

Published by Louisiana State University Press
Copyright © 2012 by David Huddle
All rights reserved
Manufactured in the United States of America
First printing

Designer: Laura Roubique Gleason
Typeface: Calluna
Printer and binder: IBT Global
LSU Press Paperback Original

Library of Congress Cataloging-in-Publication Data
Huddle, David, 1942–
  Blacksnake at the family reunion : poems / David Huddle.
    p. cm. — (Southern messenger poets)
  ISBN 978-0-8071-4469-5 (pbk. : alk. paper) — ISBN 978-0-8071-4470-1 (pdf) —
ISBN 978-0-8071-4471-8 (epub) — ISBN 978-0-8071-4472-5 (mobi)
  I. Title.
  PS3558.U287B53 2012
  811'.54—dc23

                                                            2011050509

Acknowledgments: "The Stile" appeared in *Coal Hill Review*. "Aloft" appeared in
The Southern Review. "Your Father Would Be Ashamed of You" and "This Morn-
ing" appeared in *The Hopkins Review*. "Burned Man" and "She and My Granddad"
appeared on *The Writers Almanac*. "The Anxiety of Influence" appeared in *The
Harvard Review*. "What the Stone Says" appeared in *Vantage Point*. "Mother Song"
appeared in *The Salon*. "Hilltop Sonnet" appeared in *The Southern Poetry Anthology,*
volume 3: *Contemporary Appalachia*. "Roanoke Pastorale" and "Weather Report"
appeared in *The New Yorker*. "Linguistics 101" and "Beautiful Aunt" appeared in
Subtropics. "Boy Story" appeared in *Zone 3*. "In My Other Life" appeared in *Album*.
"When I Wore a Yellow Polka Dot Dress" appeared in *South85*. "1953 Dodge
Coronet" appeared in *Appalachian Heritage*. "Strangers at Twilight" appeared in
Shenandoah.

The paper in this book meets the guidelines for permanence and durability of
the Committee on Production Guidelines for Book Longevity of the Council on
Library Resources. ∞

For my students, who for the
past forty years have refused
to let me graduate

CONTENTS

BLACKSNAKE AT THE FAMILY REUNION

BLACKSNAKE AT THE
FAMILY REUNION

Shy visitor, you've
empowered Bess who
so frightened her mom
she went up to her room—

& Molly's never seen
a snake up close, let
alone anyone grasping
such slippery magic.

That's Tara up
there on the step—
she & my nephew
divorced years

back & she fell off
the planet as far
as our family's
concerned. Bess is

fourteen here & soon
she'll set you loose
in the honeysuckle,
grateful to you

for having shown her
exactly what
she needs to know
to live in this world.

THE STILE

A stile is a pair of steps or ladders that is accessible to pedestrians but generally inaccessible to animals. Stiles are often found in rural areas or along footpaths and allow access to a field or other area enclosed by a fence or wall. Unlike a gate, there is no chance of forgetting to close it. . .
— *Wikipedia*

Between the house of my mother's childhood
and the one where my father grew up was

a field about the size of a city
block, a fence on both sides, with a gate through

which he had to pass to enter the field,
then a stile over which he had to pass

to leave the field and arrive in her yard.
My brothers and I were specks of cosmic

dust floating far above the thistles, clover,
alfalfa, and wild strawberries that grew

in that field—no bodies, brains, or spirits,
we nevertheless witnessed a young man's more

and more frequent trips through the gate, across
the field, and over the stile that summer,

both their mothers watching from bedroom windows
that faced each other across the shimmering

heat of June, July, and August. Desire
is the sky, the grass, the smell of cedar,

specks of light shooting through blackness: it knows
no authority. Our mother was fifteen,

compelling as fire seen for the first time,
strong-willed as a young horse. Their mothers knew

better than to say no. My brothers and I kept
our watch, drifting closer each time my father

approached the stile to find her on the porch,
waiting in the wicker rocker. Her half-closed

eyes saw him flying to her. That's when they
must have felt us waiting out there in time.

1953 DODGE CORONET

When my brothers & I are
      thirteen & ten & eight
      our father drives us
         & our mother to the Fair
            in Wytheville & Charles
            & Bill & I pinch each
      other while we tease
      them from the back seat.
         Is this the year you'll
            ride the Ferris Wheel,
               maybe try the Bumper Cars,
                  Scrambler, Cobra, Octopus,
                  Crazy shake, or even Ring
                     of Fire? Mother turns & winks
            at him, & still watching
            the road he turns to her
         & slyly grins & we wait to hear
      in their voices what it is
   we're after, their tone
that will tell us if we'll
be safe for another year.
   Just the Merry-Go-Round
      this time and only that
         if your dad rides with me
            Mother announces & lifts
               her chin toward him, &
                  he nods & says *Carousel*
                     will do it for me, so that
                        now we see her side-saddle
                        on the rising-falling horse,
                        him standing beside her & oh
                     how ready we feel, how we
                  jab & swat each other,

chortling like baboons,
screwing up our courage
for Kamikaze, Insanity,
Paratrooper and the one
they can't ever stand to
see us ride & so we save it
for last—the Wall of Death—
which makes Bill cry & me
scream while they wait
for us outside the gate &
then sleepy & quiet,
Bill & I each take one
of our mother's hands,
Charles pulls our father's
arm across his shoulder,
& the five of us walk
back to our car so slowly
the ride home takes us
the rest of our lives.

THIS MORNING

I'm sweet on my long-dead mother
who, when a car had knocked me down
beside the road, hoisted me up
and carried me to our back seat,

held me in her lap the whole way
to Doctor Pope's office, and stayed
with me through the long hospital
night, cooling my forehead with her hand.

Months after my cast had been cut
away and my leg was strong enough
for me to walk and run again,
it was she who noticed a boy

temporarily paralyzed
at a crosswalk in Wytheville, she
who knew the answer to the question
others must have asked themselves—

Why is that boy just standing there?
Not always the best of mothers,
that day she had it in her to step
up beside me, and as if it were

a joke, smile and take my hand and cross
the street with me. That's all it took.
When I got my confidence back,
she acted like it'd never been lost.

MOTHER SONG

your mother used to sing
you should have heard her back then
   —Abby Meunier, "Trees, like Bones"

Clothes she wore, how she loved
to sit with her sister on the back
porch steps, the two of them
grown women talking intently

as young girls, skirts hitched up
for the morning sun to warm their legs.
Things that made her cry fifty years ago,
movies she liked, men she admired,

politicians she didn't, what
a terrible driver she was, even, God
help me, what the inside of her purse
smelled like and how she shook

her car keys on her way out to the garage
as if to say *I'm going now*—
but almost no data about her
singing. Just this once, in church,

a quavering voice, shy, discernibly flat
though barely audible among all us feeble
Episcopalians more or less mutilating
"The Ties That Bind," the flattened fox

draped across the shoulders of the woman
in the pew in front of us wide awake,
eyeing us steadily, nary a blink, and I
still a boy but a man, too, deeply

moved, not understanding why,
and not wanting her to see me cry.

ALOFT

When her Alzheimer's was just beginning,
my mother had a suitor, a farmer
whose wife had died after a long illness,
a man who wanted to enjoy the years
he had left and who—so he told her—hoped
she'd help him do that. Clearly she liked
being wooed in her late sixties; she, too,
had spent a thousand hours with my father
in his dying; and in her eyes farmers
were always decent, hard-working people.
Plus the man told her he bought a new
Cadillac every year. *He's done well,*
she liked to say, lifting one eyebrow
to let us know we weren't to take him
lightly.
            We didn't.
                        My brothers and I
knew her like a textbook we'd been studying
all our lives but had never mastered—if
our inheritance was to be diverted
to a leathery old shitkicker from out
in the county, well, better somebody
like that get her money than the shyster
lawyer who sent her candy and roses
on her birthday. Vain and vulnerable,
she'd married at fifteen, had never been
courted by anybody but our father,
knew about the world mostly from movies
and books, and of course from raising three
sons, whatever a woman learns from that.
We expected the call—

                        Son, I'm married,
might be how she'd say it, or *He's asked me,
what do you think?* That would be nice of her,
asking our opinion, though she'd have made

up her mind already. When it did come,
what she said was, *We're going flying.*
Pressed for details, she said she didn't know—
he'd told her he wanted to surprise her.

Days passed, we heard nothing, my wife told me
to call. *Maybe he's kidnapped her,* she said.
I can't quite see that, I said, but I called
and instantly knew from her edgy voice
that her farmer hadn't done very well.
He took me up in a hot-air balloon,
she said. *Then he asked me. . .*
                                        I held my breath
a good minute waiting for her to tell,
but she, too, seemed to be holding her breath.
What? I asked at the same moment she said,
*Almost seventy years old, I'd never
even been in an airplane, we're hanging
up there like a cloud, I'm beside myself,
and this jackass proposes to me. . .*
                                        I cleared
my throat, but she continued: *Your father,*
she said, *would have had better sense than that.*
It made me dizzy to think of my dead
father up there with my mother—she must
have just imagined it herself, because
her voice was softer when she went on.
*In the first place he'd have never taken
me up there, but if he had, he'd at least
have waited until we were on the ground
before he popped the question.*
                                        We both stayed
quiet for a while, as if we'd brought him
back to life, and we needed a moment
to recover. Then she went on. *Your father*

would have taken me on the train. We'd have been
going somewhere.
                    And that was it—
                                her mind
stopped keeping track of what was then and what
was now. One afternoon she called the sheriff
weeping and saying she'd lost her sons,
and when he went up there, she seemed to think
it was about 1950. A year
later, she turned up on somebody's porch
in her pajamas, scratched up from walking
through briars, wild-eyed, banging on the door
after midnight with a thunderstorm raging.
Looking for somebody, said the sheriff
who called me, adding a polite chuckle
that I took to mean he knew a little more
than he was saying. *Embarrassing* was
what I first thought about that episode,
but I've changed my mind. The nursing home
we put her in is what shames me. The night
she ran through thunder and lightning, cutting
herself to ribbons, to find her mystery
lover? *Glorious* is how I see that now.

BURNED MAN

When I was twelve, a man was burned
not quite to death at my father's
factory. Recovered enough
to walk the town, he didn't know
what to do with himself—a ghost
whose scarred, fire bubbled face made you
look away, though not my father
who felt responsible and so wouldn't
refuse the man's eyes when they fell
upon him. The burned man held no
grudge, thought the accident his
own fault, and sought my father out
as the one whose eyes told him yes,
he was still alive.
                              So they held long
conversations on the post office
stoop, which I observed from the car
where I waited, where I could read
my father's stiff shoulders, the way
he clutched the mail, how he tilted
his head, even his smile that was
in truth a grimace. I knew just
what my mother knew—my father
had to let himself be tortured
once or twice a week, whenever
Bernard Sawyers saw him in town,
lifted his claw of a hand, rasped
out his greeting that sounded like
a raven that'd been taught to say
Hello, Mr. Huddle, how are you?
They'd stand there talking in the town's
blazing sunlight, the one whom fire
had taken to the edge of death
and the other invisibly
burning while they passed the time of day.

YOUR FATHER WOULD BE ASHAMED OF YOU

In her Alzheimer's fury, Mother spoke
words that kept sinking in and that now rise
randomly through my days. Peeling carrots,
walking the dog, professing ever so
wisely to attentive students, I'll hear
be ashamed and wince, or *your father*
will make me blink back tears, or *treating me
this way, you coward* will make me suddenly
need to walk home, finish off that bottle
of Old Crow, crawl under the covers,
and stay all afternoon. Mother, I'm sorry

we had to take your car keys away from you,
kidnap you from your house, put you in
the nursing home. I beg you, please don't tell—
I swear it'll never happen again.

WHAT THE STONE SAYS

. . . his life no more than the sound of his name,
the time it took to say it.
      —Irini Spanidou, *Before*

I've a sister
older than me
but whose lifespan
was mere minutes—

BORN & DIED says
her small stone, then
a single date
in November.

Seventy-two's
how old she'd be
this year. Sometimes
I write poems

about her. This time
I'm not going
to tell her name.
This time I won't

reconstruct how
it was for my
parents the day
she came and went.

Let's say I've lived
three or four books'
worth of days, then
what about her?

The ampersand
tells the whole truth
and nothing but,
so help me God,

whose divine shrug
is expressed so
eloquently
by that grave mark.

WHEN I WORE A YELLOW POLKA DOT DRESS

In the George Wythe High School auditorium,
at "The Boys' Beauty Contest" in 1958,
I played to the rowdy crowd

as best I could but got only nervous laughs,
a couple of jeers, and mostly
tepid applause.

But here's what I remember: how serious
Mary Sawyers was helping me
put on my make-up,

Nancy Umberger stuffing my bra with gym socks,
Sarah Parsons grieving over how wrong
my ballet flats

looked with that dress. T. W. Alley,
our All-State tackle who'd got
his front teeth knocked

out that year—a 260 pound bawdy slut
who turned her back to the audience
and shook it—won,

and every single one of us teenage queens
knew T. deserved it, but still—
and I don't know why nobody

ever talked about it—backstage, us boys
changing back to the sex
we were used to

and even the girls who'd helped change us—
we were all kind of quiet
and sad.

BOY STORY

Willie Crockett, my friend Sonny's mother, mothered
me through high school, when I wanted nothing

                more than to smoke cigarettes, drive fast,
              slide Melva Stephens's underpants off her hips

in the back seat of my mother's Dodge Coronet,
play my sax so gorgeously the whole world

                would bat its eyes at me when I walked down
              the hall in my pink shirt with the turned-up

collar and my black pants that'd been pegged
skin-tight by Bobby Walters's mother

                who did it as a favor to my mother,
              with whom she and Melva's mother played bridge

on Thursday afternoons, along with Eddy
Walcott's mother and Marty Kincer's mother,

                and some other mothers of kids I didn't give
              a damn about, because I was too cool

for them, focused as I was on Melva
and those knickers, which I absolutely knew

                she wanted to give up except for knowing
              her mother'd know she'd done it the very

minute she did it—and so it was me
against the invisible forces of wholesome

                behavior, which included T. W.
              Umberger's mother who went to Melva's church

and Susan Puckett's mother who recognized
the kind of boy I was when she saw me

        offer Melva a cigarette at Band camp,
         but I was winning the battle, I swear

to God, I got that lingerie started
on its life-changing journey down Melva's

      majorette thighs the night when we parked out
       by the Lutheran graveyard, with Elvis helping

me with "Love Me Tender" on the radio,
when all of a sudden Melva stopped me,

      sat up straight, and whispered, "Oh my God,
       my grandmother's buried right over there,"

got her garments back in order, rolled down
her window to get the wind to cool her face off

      so it wouldn't be just so obviously beet red
       when she had to go in to face her mom.

THICK AND THIN

Obnoxious
boy that I was,
God gave me zits
to keep me meek.

Now I've got old
person's skin—nodes
rashes, and pits,
liver-spotted

hands, batch of scars,
scaly places,
moles all over.
Melanoma

came calling once,
wants to come back.
Jane Jevons looks
me over once

every six months,
sometimes burns off
little pieces
of me. We have

certain moments,
Jane and I, eye
to eye, eerie
doctor-patient

intimacy
recognizing
I'm in my skin,
you're in yours,

but it might have
been otherwise—
this gets tricky—
my history

is what makes me
me, thank God it's
recorded here.
Me creative

writing, you derm-
atology,
we two stretchy
bags of so much

matter and just
a smattering
of what we call
consciousness.

Then Jane pulls back,
I do, too, and while
she reads the chart,
I put my shirt on.

We're much relieved
saying goodbye.
I leave, thinking
Well, it would be

all right being
Jane—she's got such
beautiful skin—
but I know she's

really happy
we didn't trade
lives. *That man's face
can't be repaired,*

she thinks. So I
in my car, she
in her office,
glance out into

space, then at
the exact same
time, we grimly
shake our skulls.

MEDICAL

While she cut the small piece out of my back
(just beneath the tendon of my shoulder),
my surgeon's breathing behind her mask

sounded oddly intimate to my ear.
I knew she'd entered the necessary trance
a doctor needs for such a procedure.

To help her focus I kept my silence,
though I'd have preferred some conversation.
Her fingers pushed and pulled to stretch my skin's

surface taut and make a clean incision.
To slow down the bleeding she cauterized
with an electric needle, so the room

stank with my own burning, but what surprised
me was how it calmed me to hear her breathe,
a soft cadence with which I synchronized

my own breathing. Her name was Elizabeth,
and I doubt she knew mine in those minutes.
Elizabeth helped David delay his death

by twenty years. It was as intense
for her as it was for me, except hers
was a magician's experience—

poof!—someone's melanoma disappears—
whereas I came away from that room
healed but estranged, as if I'd been lovers

with somebody who'd been sublimely schooled
in how sometimes flesh needs what a blade can do.

STRANGERS AT TWILIGHT

The black mare with the white diamond lets me
bump foreheads with her across the fence,
Then we're at a loss. I was lonely the whole
afternoon. All day her girl didn't come

to ride. In this field big enough for a dozen,
she's the single horse. I tell her she's pretty.
She lightly sniffs my new shirt. That's it—we're
at the end of what can transpire between an old man

and a young horse who've just met. I say goodbye,
wave as I would to my sister if I had one, then
walk down my side of the fence line. She waits
a long moment, then trots, catches up, and will

pass me except that sixty-eight years old I know
from third grade a race when I'm in one, by golly
I'm with her five strides, seven, ten! Then, well—
I let her win. She and I both know what's right.

SHE AND MY GRANDDAD

My grandfather—who died in 1970—
the year *Sexual Politics* was published—

called objects—screwdrivers, blow torches, trucks
—and sometimes even abstractions—winter,

pain, time—by the singular feminine
pronoun—*she* or *her*. For instance he would say,

I reckon she's coming up on quitting time,
or (of a favorite hammer), *I guess*

she ain't nowhere to be found. Kate Millett,
asked about the future of the woman's movement,

said, *How in the hell do I know? I don't run it,*
to which Granddad—at war with Grandmama all

my life but drawn to women, always polite—
would have said, *Yes ma'am, can't nobody run her.*

THE ANXIETY OF INFLUENCE

A long black jogger swings in off the street to
splash his face in the sink and I watch the room
become a sweet humid jungle. We crowd around
the Amazon at the watering hole, twitching our noses
like wildebeests or buffalo, snorting, rooting out
mates in the heat. I want to hump every moving thing
in this place. I want to lie down in the dry dung
and dust and twist to scratch my back. I want to
stretch and prowl and grow lazy in the shade.

  —from "The Laundromat" by Dorianne Laux

When she read this poem to an audience
of maybe a hundred and fifty writers,

it was already old to her, written some
years back, about two minutes of a morning

before she turned thirty, an invisible
episode that when it happened embarrassed

her but also felt really good remembering
it for a day or two, but then it disappeared

or sank down into the deep layers of her
memory where only dreams could fetch it up—

or the occasion of writing something,
which was what desire was becoming for her

now that she was a mother, crazy busy
all day long and that old outlaw had no time

for her except some early mornings he'd drop
by while she sipped her coffee, sit with her

at her old kitchen table, and hum softly
while she fiddled with a poem, which was when

that almost nothing arose in her and became
words penciled on a notepad, erased and marked

through like a kid had just fooled around instead
of doing her homework, and it took her back

to the way she'd felt that day, blushing for her
thoughts, but it was also like she'd made the whole

thing up, and she wasn't sure it was worth keeping,
but she typed it into her computer, changed

it until she couldn't change it anymore,
and finally sent it out, which was how it

officially became a poem: How it looked
in print pleased her, no matter that it wasn't

Prufrock or *The Bridge* or even *This Is Just
to Say,* never mind that it said what she knew

she'd never have said aloud or that it wasn't
what really happened: It was the boldest truth

of her, and there it was, spoken forever
and not to be erased. So when she read it

to all these writers, and one of them stood up
just after she'd quietly sounded the words

I want to hump every moving thing and left
the room, she never faltered, her voice held

so steady it was like she hadn't even
seen him, but she had, she knew him, knew his poems,

had learned from him as if he'd been her teacher,
and that was the exact moment that she knew

she could say she was a poet without a shred
of doubt, and it was God damn thrilling for it

to happen while that poem was flowing up
over her tongue, out of her mouth, out to all

those writers sitting there listening to her—
though something in her wanted to call to him,

the old man, walking across the lawn away
from her, wanted to catch up to him, take hold

of his arm, and say, *Hey, brother, please don't take
offense, it's just a little something I made up.*

NARCOTIC

It hardly had to do with her.
    —Robert Hass, "Meditation at Lagunitas"

This woman—I'll call her Kate
—told me she discovered men
couldn't give her up once
she took a liking to them,

and once that had happened,
the man had started coming
back to her again and again,
with that half-lidded look

like please don't tell me
to go away, I need to be
around you, once he'd shown
her it wasn't affection

he felt, or the beginning
of love, or even anything
like aesthetic appreciation,
it was just plain old naked

need—why then, right that
instant, Kate could hardly
bear the fellow, no matter
his money or his charm, she

could feel it turn in her
like car sickness, the way
all of a sudden you realize
you're about to throw up,

and she'd immediately have
to put distance between
herself and him, she'd have
to run from the room, or get

out of the car. She said
once she said excuse me,
stood up from a restaurant
table, walked straight out

the door of the place, caught
a cab back to her apartment,
and never saw the guy again.
"You can't believe how much

I cared for that man—
I'd thought finally
I'd found the friend
I'd wanted since I was

ten years old and played
with Tommy Swecker across
the street and he and I
told each other secrets

under his back porch,
and this man was like
that, somebody I wanted
to tell my whole life to,

but then he reached
across the table, put two
fingers to the inside
of my wrist like he was

taking my pulse, and it
just freaked me out, I
knew the woman he had
in his mind wasn't me,

and knew he was so hooked
on her, he'd make her
miserable before he'd
give her up." Kate and I

both lived in California
then, I had a place
in Del Mar, she lived
down near Torrey Pines,

and that's where we'd meet,
at that park—we'd agreed
to meet every Saturday
morning at 10:30

at a bench up on the bluff
that looked down the coast
almost to Mexico, and God,
the conversations we had

up there! I even joked
to myself about how she
and I met in Heaven once
a week, which I thought

would amuse her, and it did
make her laugh that morning
so that I hoped she'd tell
me her address, maybe let me

come to her place for coffee,
nothing really threatening,
I knew better than that,
but I'd realized I was never

happier than when we were
talking up on that bluff,
staring out at the Pacific,
where her voice was this rich

alto that swear to God made
me hear her every word
like it was newly uttered
in the world, I even knew

better than to look at her
face while she talked,
because I knew I'd be lost
then, and that morning,

I don't know how she
figured it out, but all
of a sudden, she stood up
from the bench, pushed

the hair out of her eyes,
blinked at me maybe
a couple of times, turned
and walked toward the trail

back down the bluff,
and you might ask me why
I didn't call to her
or follow her, or make

some kind of effort not
to lose her—that would be
a fair question—why not
at least try to save what

we had? but it was like
this at the time, and it's
like this now, I knew it
wasn't *we* at all, it was

what *I* had, it was like she
triggered something in my
brain, and so watching her
walk down that path, her hair

swirling in that California
sunlight, I understood it
wasn't Kate needing to escape,
it was me needing to let her go.

HARD DRIVE

My friend—husband of the woman I love—
told me a story of their married life:
Before they had children, they often drove

the interstate at night. He said his wife
liked to lie down with her head in his lap
and then ask him these random questions, like

what he did in first grade, did he like soup,
what was his first girlfriend's name, did her mom
keep an eye on them, what made them break up. . .

My friend said they were the kind of questions
that had him talking like he never talked
anyplace but in the car with her. One

hand steered while the other hand sort of stroked
her arm, her hip, her breast, sometimes her face.
He said it was strange, he kept his eyes locked

on the highway while his mind tried to trace
down the answers to her questions, but then
something else was going on, too—this space

opened up where his wife could be with him
just so intimately it almost freaked
him out, but then she also seemed to be in

her own world, too. He kept a steady speed
and let her put his hand wherever she
wanted it. Sometimes he'd sneak a quick peek,

but he knew she didn't want him to see
her open blouse, loosened bra, hiked-up skirt,
especially her face in that strange green

radiance. My friend said he knew his first
job was to drive, his second was to string
out sentence after sentence, and his third

wasn't a real job, it was just lending
her a hand, so to speak. He said she gave
him an education. Then the children

came along. "Used to say, 'Let's take a drive,'
we hopped in the car and went. Same words now
mean 'try to get a baby-sitter.' We've

forgotten the words, we've had to learn how
to live such completely different lives
we're like actors cast in another show."

He shakes his head and makes a face. "I love
my kids," he says. "Don't get me wrong. Love her,
too, I guess, even if I can't say I have

the same sense of her that used to be there—
just right there!—at seventy-five miles an hour
straight up the interstate in a dark car."

My friend broods over his drink. "Know what our
problem is?" I ask him. I sometimes wonder
how much he knows. "Your wife is the flower

of my eye, as you no doubt know"—I under-
cut these words with irony so he'll think
I'm kidding—"but we can hardly stand her

as your basic human being, a unit
without sex or desire, just another
pipe that turns food into excrement."

"You've got a way with words, don't you, brother?"
he says. "Sure, we all get to be the pipe
eventually. I can't send the mother

of my kids to a nursing home or wipe
out that old file in my computer just
now. Did I ever tell you how contrite

and kind she was when she was all finished,
weepy and apologetic while I looked
for a place to turn around? 'I'm selfish,'

she'd say. 'I'm sorry, it's just that I'm hooked
on your sexy voice.' She'd sit up and fix
her clothes. Then she'd whisper, 'But you're in luck,

because we've got quite a few miles betwixt
here and home, and I'm ready to take you
where you just took me.' Moving over next

to me, she'd rest her hand on my thigh, move
her fingers ever so slightly. 'Great place
to go—I guarantee you'll like it, too.'

I'd look in the rearview, check out my face,
try to guess if I was lying. 'I'd rather wait
till we get home,' I'd say. So a silence

would fall and stay in the car all the way
back, but she'd keep her hand there, her fingers
letting me know they knew the final say

was right there in my pants. We didn't linger
in the car, we'd race from the garage, clothes
flying all through the house, we'd fling our

underwear off in the dark, never close
the curtains, and hit the bed, no foreplay
necessary. No wonder we got those

kids the way we did. No wonder those days
are over and done with. I just wonder
how she could disappear without a trace.

It's not my blushing bride I want back—her
smile drove me nuts anyway. That hussy
in the car is who I want to return."

"She's waiting at the nursing home," I sigh.
He snorts. "Not there yet, buddy, though you keep
trying to put us there." "I feel like I

lost her, too," I tell him. Sure, I'm a creep
for drinking with him like this just to hear
him talk about his wife. I'd never sleep

with the woman—she's just way too sincere
for my taste. But it's knowing what she is
now that makes the way my pal remembers

her so necessary for both of us.
I don't think the situation's dangerous.

IN MY OTHER LIFE

You make me laugh like an idiot
—NQ Arbuckle

Me & my sweetie live like this
almost always at least a little
jacked up very fashion-hostile
not particularly hygienic needing

sleep but entirely too wired even
to nap semi-outraged & bemused
by this brain-dead town & each other
on account of how everything's

out of sync—like the fact that
we're late now & it's hard to find
a credit card between us that isn't
maxed out & drivers' licenses

& fifty dollar bills keep falling
out of my pockets & her purse & no
restaurant will give us a table
but my sweetie's still got enough

of her looks left & still remembers
what it takes to flirt the starch
out of any stuffed shirt & so we make
do fake it & make it up hour by hour

& so what if this motel room smells
like it was last slept in by a water
buffalo & a hyena you just hand me
a microphone play me a four-bar intro

to something in B-Flat I'll start crooning
whatever's in the mood to float down
from my brain & out across my tongue
& it'll be so edgy & melodious

the crowd will throw cash at us
my sweetie will scramble down & scoop
it off the floor she'll glance back
up at me from down there & invite me

to come down & participate in the harvest
& I'll tell her she looks like either
a train or an airplane wreck I don't
know which & she'll tell me to shut

my spout & get down there with her
or she'll rip off her mask & reveal
she's actually my Methodist mother
come back from the dead & I'll laugh

like an idiot & for the next five
minutes scuffling for our livelihood
down there on the floor we'll be happier
than about six thousand normal people.

THE HUSBAND'S TALE

... the difficult signs for flight, for
danger, as well as the simpler one
for love

— "Adam Signing," by John Engels

1.

I know what they say—it was her silence
I married her for. They've got it right. She's
never spoken. She has no voice box,
so she can't even hum to herself. Yes,

she can write—her elegant hand can fly
across a page, every sentence crackling
with intelligence and passion for life,
the world and its creatures, books, art, music—

and when she signs, people gather around
her as if her hands and fingers reveal
how we came to be here, what we must do
with our lives, and what happens after we

die. No matter they can't read her gestures.
They want what I want. To listen anyway.

2.

Forty years we've been companions—a long,
intricate dance begun the day we met.
In high school, someone said, *That new girl can't
talk,* and I went to see her for myself.

So her stillness was the first fact I knew
about her. Her looks were ordinary—
no one said she was pretty—but her face
had a kind of power. Kids got quiet

around her, and if she looked straight at you,
it could make you shiver. She and I locked
eyes that first day, and nowadays we joke
that was the moment we made our wedding vows.

She was voted our commencement speaker.
Beside her, I read her speech. Sounded her words.

3.

Never a man, but when women see us
together—their faces say it—they suspect
a talking husband with a silent wife.
Like it's a new sexual perversion.

They might not be wrong. When Ruth Ann and I
make love, it's the words I say that excite
her, the flutter and caress of her hands
and fingers that move me along with her.

Is this too intimate? Well, there you have it—
The other side of power is a cool,
secret place, a meadow where two can go
to lie down in smooth grass to spend hours.

A fingertip brushing along the skin
inside a wrist. *Just you* whispered like *Amen.*

4.

Yes, children. And yes, they must have suffered
difficulty and embarrassment they
never even told us about, schoolmates
with hands over their mouths mocking Ruth Ann,

exaggerating the long stare at a face
that's become my habit. Robert's oldest,
Michelle only a year younger. They're sweet
kids and never told us of any trouble

we might have caused them. School's where you find out
how the world views your parents. They brought home
friends, and the friends watched us. We know they had
their thoughts. But somehow we passed inspection.

Once we even chaperoned a school dance,
danced the jitterbug for them—but just once.

5.

Once, furious, her hands seemed to explode:
You use silence against me! It's not fair!
I must have blinked, because her mouth opened
like that agonized person's in Munch's *The Scream*—

and she made the same sound the painting makes—none
whatsoever. It was just so eerie!
Married a few years, we suddenly saw
that navigating love all right didn't

mean we could handle fear and rage. I don't
know how I knew to do this, don't remember
deciding to do it, just knew to drop
straight to the floor, kneel, hug her knees, bury

my head, and say, "I'm so sorry!" When I
looked up, she smiled and signed, *Keep talking.*

6.

My worst fear was she'd be hurt somewhere near
and I'd be oblivious. More and more
I'd go check on her wherever I thought
she was—gardening, ironing, watching TV.

I got so I could do it without her
noticing, just a glance from a window
or through a door, but in the course of years
I realized she knew almost every

time but pretended not to notice. What
this says about marriage or the two of us
I don't know, but once when she sat reading
in the back yard sunlight, I passed the porch door

like a ghost spying on a statue, then
stepped back and caught that slight to-herself grin.

7.

Gardening would be only the general
term for what she did with flowers, trees, rocks,
water, grass, shrubs, even daylight and shadow.
It took years for me to see how the odd

little pieces of land around our house
had evolved into a park for ghosts or
angels, or maybe it was outsider art
for a few discerning pedestrians

who could recognize arrangements she'd changed
dozens of times—buried hoses made fountains,
one that washed down a rock face into a pool
lined with stones she'd found, a miniature

grotto with a bench beneath soft Chinese
chimes that called *Come sit down in paradise.*

8.

One more won't hurt. Saying it swung open
the door to *Les Bon Temps*—and Ruth Ann tipsy
was funnier than a dozen speaking
women. "You're slurring your words," I'd tell her,

and she'd gesture gibberish and cross her
eyes. Oh, we said it a lot in those years
before the night I hip-checked her across
the kitchen and broke her wrist.

                                        What had seemed

only giddy pleasure turned in that instant
to a drunken husband (me) abusing
his disadvantaged wife (Ruth Ann), waking
their sleeping kids with his violent act.

Right hand in a cast. The left didn't feel
like talking, and our sad silence a jail.

9.

One Monday morning at Dunkin' Donuts
I realized I was pointing at what
I wanted. I actually forced myself
to say *Thank you* to the woman counting

change into my palm. I sat in the car
a long while, thinking about when I'd last
spoken aloud. As if they were someone
else's, my hands signed—*Friday afternoon*

at work. Kids away at school, with the house
to ourselves, Ruth Ann and I, without
ever agreeing it was what we wanted,
had given ourselves over to silence.

Or maybe released it from the basement,
attic, and closets. Treated it like a guest.

WEATHER REPORT

The vultures of this landscape came to call
this morning—found a bare-limbed tree outside
my kitchen window, settled in & held
my gaze, big tar blobs against a milky sky:
We understand you, their presence informed me,
& *I you,* I told them in silence.
                                        Right now
this day can't make up its mind—sun's half out
but rain's in those clouds. If it's that cold wind-
driven stuff that swats your eyes like a drink
full of crushed ice thrown in your face, I'll stay
indoors, count my failures & petty crimes,
loathe my life, & completely understand
why friends and loved ones keep their distance.
The barometer yo-yos my mental state—
one day I'm a happy old dude, kitchen
dancer, car-driving harmonizer, hilltop
walker delighted by the world.
                                        Next day
it's the big not, the mega-never. & where
are you breeze-blown death birds now that I need you?
This mean rain's rotting the starch right out of me.
Come down from your perch, my beauties, I'm
opening doors & windows, I'm looking for snacks
in the back of the fridge. Here—try roosting
on this chair back. Please just sit with me
around my table. I'll hold up both ends
of our conversation. It's like forever
I've wanted to talk to you. Here—let me
turn off these lights—I know you like the dark.

HILLTOP SONNET

Who visits this high meadow, lawn of the dead,
  to see blue and bluer mountains that rise
    out of the west; to converse with the crows,
      great-winged turkey buzzards, black kites riding
        thermals in seamless silence; to greet deer
          here at twilight grazing near the wood's edge;
            to scare the huge groundhog that lives inside
              the brick-walled graveyard: Who moves through this space?

      A yellow dog leading a deaf old man
        who likes to talk, a girl and her boyfriend
          who sit atop her car's roof murmuring
            quietly, two off-leash labs ignoring
          their shouting owner, a policeman who
        parks up here to feel lonely, guarding the wind.

ROANOKE PASTORALE

Cardinal, goldfinch, titmouse, turkey buzzard—
dear companions of my afternoons—
above this field, high clouds dream of blizzards

to snow me in till spring ends my solitude.
Sober's my binge now, nature my saloon.
Wren, mourning dove, house finch, turkey buzzard—

for your entertainment, I sing the words
of old fifties songs, use baby talk, croon
as I walk the field beneath great blizzard-

dreaming clouds. You gaudy pretties, sweet birds
of my senior years—my later's my soon.
Catbirds flit through cedars in the graveyard,

turkey buzzards swirl their patterns overhead,
across the mountainside sunlight bows a tune
rising to blue eternity but heard

by the heron fishing the creek, wizard
of stillness, creature designed by the moon.
Bluebird, jay, chipping sparrow, turkey buzzard,
clouds, and field—I dream this life, walk this world.

LINGUISTICS 101

In *friend* lies *end,*
the dark edge of
any friendship:
People quarrel,

death takes this one
or that, or else
distance will make
them *distant friends—*

altogether
dissimilar.
In *love* lies the
poetic *O,*

as in *O, sweet
face, frown hast thou
never known,* and
so on, whereas

in marriage
lie *mar* and *age,*
words of warning
to the fickle,

and cautious.
*Why would I want
to be tarnished
and then get old?*

Let's just be friends.
Others marry,
find the *O ends*
quick as lightning.

Some few hitch up,
take their marring,
their aging, too.
They get beat up

by each other,
their kids, and time.
Sure, it's ugly—
God will smack you

around any
way you play it.
Get lucky, though,
and find yourself—

you've seen these folks—
an old couple
out on the town,
wine to drink, food

to eat, music
to hear, and yes,
maybe dancing's
not so easy

for them, but two
talking forty
years make a kind
of poetry.

They're in it
until it ends.
Reaper's mounted
and on the way—

God knows what else—
while they laugh and
raise their glasses,
to toast nothing

we'd understand.
But can't we say
they resemble
old friends in love?

BEAUTIFUL AUNT

Our beautiful Aunt Constance rejected
suitors almost recreationally,
spoke with flamboyance, and behaved
with such charming peculiarity

she was much loved in our town. One Sunday
dinner she announced, "I have far too many
friends," then commenced eating her peas one
at a time. A mild April afternoon,

dusk just coming on, the breeze wafting
through the dining room windows, stirring mother's
lace curtains: We studied her face. "Also
I've fallen in love," she murmured. "Oh Connie,"

our mother said, "I'm so happy for you."
Our father grinned—he knew more was coming.
Our aunt lifted her eyes and said, "The wedding
will be next Sunday. Just the family."

She excused herself then though dinner had
just begun. She was almost to the stairs when
our father called out, "Who's the lucky guy?" Her
brother, he knew her best of any of us, though

my brothers and I were her loyal subjects.
"The copper beech," she said, stopped in the hallway,
gone dreamy for a moment. We knew the tree
she meant, high and lonely, a deep purple tent

of a thing that looked like it had been dropped
from a space ship and speared down into the hilltop
of Sisks' pasture, a circle of shade so thick
sunlight never touched the ground underneath it.

It was where we always went for picnics, so
familiar to us it made sense our aunt
had chosen it. My brothers and I knew it
was strange and kind of a joke, but not one

of us questioned the need to give our aunt
what she wanted. This was years ago, but it's
still vivid in our minds. The ceremony
was so solemn and funny and correct

it has become the story we know and tell
among ourselves, our cherished family
riddle, the test for anyone who thinks
of joining the bond of our whimsical blood.

We make a point of telling fiancés how
Aunt Constance wore a gown of brown satin
with a green veil, and carried a wild swatch
of forsythia, how our father read

the service in his booming voice, how
our mother was a sweetly tearful matron
of honor, and how my savage brothers
and I stood in the sunlight, our shirts off

and our skin painted purple and bright orange.
When our father asked our beautiful aunt
if she took this tree for her husband, she
whispered that she did, she certainly did.

When our father turned to the tree and asked
if it took this woman for its wife, a breeze
rose up, shifted its limbs slightly, fluttered
its leaves, and brought forth the old shadowy

scent of copper beech we had known all our lives.
Grandparents, aunts and uncles, cousins, brothers
and sisters, small children running in and out
of the great tree's shade—we picnicked through

the long afternoon, then our Aunt Constance
delivered a short speech to us, at the end
of which she made a special request: "To honor
my new husband I ask that you all roll down

this magnificent hill." No sooner had
she asked it than we began getting down
on all fours, lying down and pushing ourselves
sideways down the slope, even our mother

who giggled for years afterward whenever
she remembered how our beautiful aunt
stood in the shade of her copper beech,
laughing and laughing at her foolish family.